AI in Real Estate
Predictive Analytics, Valuation, and Investment

Table of Contents

Chapter 1. Introduction

In this Special Report, we explore an intersection where the future meets tradition: Artificial Intelligence (AI) in Real Estate. From predictive analytics that fine-tune property valuations and forecast market fluctuations, to AI-fuelled investment strategies altering the landscape of property finance, this arena is brimming with innovation. However, this is not merely a futuristic vision for realty speculation. It's happening right now, revolutionizing the way we buy, sell, and think about property. Don't worry if you're not an AI-whizz - we've pillared this report on clarity and accessibility. So, take a step into tomorrow and discover how AI is reshaping real estate, and find out why you might want to lever this transformative technology in your portfolio. You're just one read away from being on the cutting edge of property investment evolution. Excited? Us too. Let's begin the journey together.

Chapter 2. Introduction to AI in Real Estate

Artificial Intelligence (AI), and its subset machine learning, are driving a new age of innovation and productivity in virtually every sector, and the real-estate industry is no exception. While AI may suggest images of robots and self-driving cars, the reality is a series of algorithms and data-crunching capabilities have started to influence the property sector in ways no less transformative.

2.1. How AI is Changing the Real Estate Landscape

AI-powered solutions are now transforming nearly every segment of the real estate industry, from investment to sales, valuation, and financing, with three primary models: predictive analytics, machine learning algorithms, and natural language processing.

1. Predictive Analytics: This involves the use of historical data, statistical algorithms, and machine learning techniques to predict future outcomes. Real estate industries employ predictive analytics to forecast housing values, future property demand, and more.

2. Machine Learning Algorithms: Machine learning assists in gauging property values by framing intelligent property-pricing models which can analyze multiple parameters including location, property type, local amenities, etc.

3. Natural Language Processing: NLP is making real estate searches easier by interpreting and responding to human language and voice commands, thereby enhancing customer experience.

The implementation of AI in the real estate industry is bringing about significant changes in how the industry operates. We'll look into these changes in the next few sections.

2.2. Why AI Matters in Real Estate

In real estate markets, time and information are of utmost value - the faster you know, the faster you act and the better your returns can be. Herein lies the power of AI, to process vast amounts of data quickly, more accurately, and dialed to specific requirements, thus enabling real estate professionals and investors to make informed decisions at an unprecedented pace.

In the industry, whether it is understanding property values, forecasting future trends, precisely targeting advertisements, or streamlining the buying process, AI can act as a catalyst, providing solutions that can enhance efficiency, reduce costs, and improve customer experiences.

For example, traditional property valuation methods are usually centered around comparables and local market knowledge. However, AI-driven platforms can create valuation models that triangulate thousands of data points, including those outside the realm of traditional real estate data. This generates a far more accurate and real-time value for properties.

2.3. Real World Applications of AI in Real Estate

Companies are already reaping the rewards of integrating AI into their products and services, and customers are benefitting from moves towards automated services. Let's discuss some real-world applications of AI in the real estate sector.

1. Property Search: AI-powered property search engine can streamline the process significantly. By understanding the user's

requirements from past searches, these engines can deliver personalized results.

2. Virtual Tours: AI-powered chatbots have revolutionized virtual property tours. They can navigate around properties using 360-degree photos and answer potential buyer's queries, making the real estate buying process smooth, even from remote distances.

3. Risk Assessment: AI can analyze multiple factors influencing a property's risk factor, including neighborhood crime rates, flood zones, property age, etc. This makes it a potent tool for investors and insurers alike.

4. Property Management: AI is making property management easier by predicting maintenance issues before they become dire, saving landlords and property managers' time and money.

5. Investment Decisions: AI and machine learning models can assess various factors such as location, community statistics, area development plans, and historical data to predict property appreciation rates, helping investors make informed decisions.

As promising as these already are, we must also address what lies ahead, potential pitfalls, and the question of ethics as we navigate our way forward.

2.4. Potential Challenges and Ethical Dilemmas

While the advantages of AI in real estate are remarkable, there are potential challenges to bear in mind. A significant concern is about the reliability of AI algorithms. If the algorithms are trained on insufficient or biased data, they risk causing misguided or discriminatory decisions. The real estate professionals must ensure transparency while employing AI and machine learning models.

Moreover, the increasing AI involvement in real estate brings up a possible ethical dilemma. There are rising concerns about job displacement. However, experts argue that AI would predominantly help in automating the mundane aspects of jobs, allowing human workers to focus on more critical and complex tasks.

2.5. Unleashing the Future

We are at an exciting crossroad where automation and AI are poised to revolutionize traditional ways we interact with the property market. AI is more than just a buzzword. It's a transformative technology that stands to radically reshape the real estate sector. Understanding this evolution and engaging with it is no longer optional, it's a necessity.

In the following chapters, we will delve deeper into this theme, uncovering the actual workings of AI in different areas of the real estate industry. Whether you are a seasoned investor, property manager, realtor, or simply interested in the future of real estate, stay tuned as we turn the pages of this vibrant chronicle of AI in real estate.

Chapter 3. Predictive Analytics: A New Perspective on Market Trends

Predictive analytics has taken center stage in the world of real estate. Its potential to decipher patterns from past data and use it to predict future outcomes makes it a game-changing technology. For investors, brokers, and even individual home buyers or sellers, this approach provides fresh insights into market trends, property valuations, and potential risks associated with various transactions.

3.1. Understanding the Basics of Predictive Analytics

Predictive Analytics is a subfield of data analytics and uses statistical algorithms and machine-learning techniques to identify the likelihood of future outcomes based on historical data. By making things clearer, faster, and better, predictive analytics can ultimately help real estate investors manage risks, reduce costs, and maximize returns.

The process of predictive analytics involves several steps. First, data is collected from numerous sources like economic indicators, housing datasets, and demographic statistics. This data is then processed, cleaned, and transformed into a usable format. Subsequently, predictive models are built using this data, which are then trained and tested on a subset of the data. These models can help generate predictions for new data.

3.2. Impact of Predictive Analytics on Real Estate

Predictive analytics can greatly impact the real estate world in several ways. Let's examine some of them:

1. **Property Valuation**: Accurate property valuation is a critical aspect of real estate. By leveraging predictive analytics, property values can be estimated more accurately using various data points like location, size, and other characteristics. This eliminates the guesswork and hunch-based decisions, making way for data-driven strategies.

2. **Market Predictions**: Predictive analytics can help anticipate market trends. For instance, it might predict a rise or fall in property prices in a particular location based on historical data, enabling investors to make informed decisions.

3. **Risk Management**: It can help identify potential risk factors such as depreciation, neighborhood crime rates, or environmental hazards. This aids in risk assessment and mitigation, critical for anyone involved in real estate investments.

3.3. Effective Use of Predictive Analytics in Investment Strategies

Investors desire to stay ahead of the curve and predictive analytics provides that opportunity. It allows investors to make critical decisions about where, when, and at what price to buy or sell a property. Here's how:

1. **Anticipating Market Trends**: By estimating how various factors will affect a property's value, predictive analytics offers a glimpse into the future. For instance, it can help anticipate if the property prices in a certain neighborhood are expected to rise significantly

in the future.

2. **Mitigating Risks**: It aids in identifying potential risks associated with a property. For example, predicted increases in the local crime rate or unexpected infrastructure developments can affect property values adversely.

3. **Balancing Portfolio**: Predictive analytics can help investors maintain a balanced portfolio. It can guide investors in deciding whether to invest more in residential properties versus commercial ones, or vice-versa.

3.4. Challenges and Limitations of Predictive Analytics

While the use of predictive analytics in real estate comes with several advantages, it is not without challenges:

1. **Accuracy of Predictions**: The accuracy of the predictions heavily depends on the quality of the historical data used. Poor data quality can lead to inaccurate results.

2. **Analytical Skills**: Application of predictive analytics requires considerable expertise in statistics, machine-learning algorithms, and other technology-related skills, which might not be the skills traditionally associated with real estate.

3. **Ethical Concerns**: Though not specific to real estate, predictive analytics also brings up a host of ethical questions about data privacy, bias in datasets, and algorithm transparency.

3.5. The Future of Predictive Analytics in Real Estate

Despite the challenges, the future of predictive analytics in real estate looks promising. The technology is constantly being refined and enhanced to make predictions even more accurate. This will allow for faster, smoother transactions, better decision-making, and increased profits for everyone involved in the sector.

Predictive analytics has the potential to revolutionize the way we understand and operate within the real estate market. Its ability to bring a new perspective on market trends and add a competitive edge is an asset stakeholders can't ignore. In the end, one thing is certain: the application of predictive analytics in real estate is set to grow, and those who can harness its power will be the ones shaping the future of the industry.

Chapter 4. AI in Property Valuation: Upping the Accuracy

Property valuation is a critical aspect of real estate transactions that dictates everything from selling prices to insurance premiums to property tax assessments. Traditionally, these valuations have relied heavily on the expertise and judgment of human appraisers. However, thanks to advances in AI, an enhanced level of accuracy and efficiency is being brought to this field. And this is just the beginning point of our probe into the matter.

4.1. The Traditional Process of Property Valuation

Let's set the stage by briefly discussing the traditional property valuation process. Real estate appraisal or property valuation is a method of creating an opinion of value for real property. The traditional property valuation process involves an appraiser visiting the property, surveying it and using their expertise to evaluate its worth based on factors such as location, age, design quality, and recent comparable sales in the neighborhood. To make a reliable valuation, it takes many hours of research and calculation.

Though this method has frequently proven effective, it isn't without its flaws. This manual process is inherently slow, expensive and is vulnerable to human error.

4.2. AI-led Transformation of Property Valuation

Now, imagine a world where property valuation is automated, rapid, and highly accurate; a world where the value of a house can be reasonably pinpointed based on millions of data points collected over years, from comparable sales, demographic shifts, and local facilities, and automatically updated as new information surfaces. This is the vision AI is bringing to life in the realm of property valuation. AI algorithms, given enough quality data, can perform a similar task to human appraisers and do so instantaneously and continuously.

Operating at a conceptually similar level to human appraisers, AI valuation models consider various property and neighborhood features such as a property's size, age, materials used, location, and proximity to facilities like schools, supermarkets, and hospitals. Beyond this, AI models can also access and incorporate a diverse range of data into their valuations than humans could practically manage—transaction data, demographic factors, even satellite imagery data to analyze the condition and appearance of a property.

4.3. Predictive Analytics: The Game Changer

At the heart of AI-powered property valuation is predictive analytics. Predictive analytics use algorithms, statistical techniques, and machine learning to analyze and predict future outcomes based on historical data. Essentially, predictive analytics has the potent ability to 'learn' from patterns identified in the past and project them onto the future.

Within the realm of property valuation, predictive analytics allows for superior accuracy by considering data from macro to micro levels. Market trends are influenced by a plethora of factors, all of which predictive analytics can dissect, extrapolate and feed into its valuation model. The adoption of predictive analytics technology is a significant step toward property valuation that is more comprehensive, reliable, and quick.

It's worth noting that predictive analytics models aren't designed to replace human appraisers completely, but rather enhance their capabilities. These models can handle the bulk of data analysis, allowing appraisers to focus on insights, evaluations, and strategies.

4.4. The Machine Learning Insight in Property Valuation

Machine learning (ML), a subset of AI, is a critical component of predictive analytics. ML models can process enormous amounts of data, much more than any human could in a lifetime, and identify patterns and correlations that might go unnoticed by the human eye.

In property valuation, this can mean capturing and evaluating complex interconnected factors that play significant roles in shaping a property's value. Variables such as the local economy's status, changing demographics, new infrastructural or policy shifts, right down to minute details like the architectural style of the neighborhood, can all be swiftly assessed by machine learning models.

Moreover, machine learning models are inherently self-improving, which means they get better at predicting property values over time as they continuously learn from new data. As new information comes to light or as market conditions evolve, ML algorithms can quickly adapt and adjust their valuation models accordingly.

4.5. Conclusion: Future of Property Valivation with AI

AI-powered property valuation promises to enhance accuracy, efficiency, and objectivity, and it's only getting started. We're already seeing the impact of AI-enhanced valuation in providing more precise and fair estimates, not to mention the time and cost savings from the automation.

However, it's important to note that AI is not about replacing the human aspect of property valuation; it's about empowering professionals with more accurate information and more time to focus on the strategic and complex parts of their jobs.

Innovation in AI technology continues to advance at a rapid clip, and its adoption in real estate and property valuation, in particular, is set to transform the industry. With every passing day, AI reinforces its value proposition, not only enhancing the quality of existing processes but also enabling new methods and strategies that promise to revolutionize how we value property. As we continue to delve into AI innovations, the future of property valuation does indeed appear very bright.

Chapter 5. Transforming Investments: AI's Role in Property Finance

As we delve into the realm of property finance, with its intricate patterns and complex algorithms, the disruptive power of AI sets the stage for profound transformation. As our economies globalize, and data becomes the new gold, an inevitable change takes place in the way we make transactions, valuations, investments, and projections about future market trends.

5.1. Adoption of AI in Property Finance

Artificial Intelligence's application in property finance represents the outcome of this change. With AI, one can gather vast amounts of data, analyze it, and make predictions or decisions based on the outcomes. This could be as simple as determining whether a potential property is worth investing in, to analyzing the risk and potential ROI of property portfolios.

These digital algorithms can sift through more than property prices - they take into account a whole wealth of data, including local market conditions, demographic trends, economic indicators, proximities to utilities and amenities, etc., to make accurate predictions about the property's future value that a human might overlook.

AI can also automate the loan approval and underwriting process, using machine learning algorithms to assess the creditworthiness of clients, determine suitable loan terms, and even predict the possibility of default based on a multitude of variables. This way, lenders can make informed decisions, manage risks better, and improve their overall operational efficiency.

5.2. AI and Investment Strategies

AI in property finance also breathes life into investment strategies. AI platforms can identify property hotspots based on trends and indicators that might go unnoticed by human investors, thus leading to better profits and lower risks.

Through predictive analytics, AI can give investors an edge by forecasting property market fluctuations, providing ample time to adjust strategies and optimize returns. For instance, if AI algorithms predict a slump in the property market, investors can either hold off buying or negotiate for a better deal. Alternatively, if AI detects a surge, investors can fast-track purchase decisions to take advantage of the bullish market trend.

Additionally, AI algorithms help in creating dynamic pricing models by analyzing past and current data related to property value, location, neighborhood development, economic climates, and potential market disruptions. Such models assist investors in making informed decisions, prevent overpricing or underpricing, and ensure maximum return on investment.

5.3. Impact of AI on Real Estate Agents and Brokers

Not to overlook the essential role of intermediaries, AI has ushered in a new era for real estate agents and brokers. It has provided tools that streamline activities, improve accuracy, and limit human error. These tools include automated property valuing, document handling, online consultations, and virtual property tours.

With the help of AI, property agents can now accurately predict market trends, understand customer behavior, and tailor services according to individual customer needs. This helps them in staying relevant amidst the increasing competition and ensures they provide optimum value to their clients.

5.4. Challenges Awaiting AI Adoption

While AI opens up a realm of fascinating possibilities, the transition is not devoid of challenges. Concerns over data privacy, lack of standardization in AI application, a dearth of skilled professionals and the cost of implementation, together pose a considerable stumbling block to seamless AI integration in property finance.

Moreover, the repercussions of AI errors can contribute to market losses, impacting investors, realtors, and proprietors alike. Therefore, it is essential to build robust AI systems that are transparent, accountable, and regulated to avoid any potential adverse effects.

5.5. Future Prospects: The AI Transformation

Lastly, the influence of AI in property finance is only set to grow bigger. With vast data resources and improved analytic capabilities, AI holds the potential to construct detailed investment strategies, precisely value properties, and project market trends with impressive accuracy.

The AI transformation is not only limited to simplifying tasks and automating processes. In the truest sense, it is reshaping the foundations of property finance. Bank credit assessments, property appraisals, investment strategies, risk management – facets that were once handled with traditional methods are now being revolutionized.

In sum, with AI's potential to streamline and optimize, it will not only serve to help those involved in the industry to realize better profits and minimize risks but also serve as an enabler for an equitable and efficient market system.

With these factors in mind, it's evident that AI is much more than a technological advancement. It holds the key to optimally managing investment portfolios and will play a catalytic role in setting the future course of property finance.

Chapter 6. Case Studies: AI Triumphs in the Real Estate Market

In the continuously evolving world of real estate, AI has been leaving its mark, and nowhere more so than in the market itself. Let's explore some real-world applications and successes that will make the impact of AI clear as glass.

6.1. AI in Property Valuation

AI's predictive capabilities have been a game-changer in property valuation. Instead of employing traditional methods, like comparing properties or manual assessments, AI systems have started to implement complex algorithms to predict property values efficiently, accurately, and in real time. This type of real-time valuation drastically reduces the time to sell or rent a property and optimizes the pricing to ensure the best value is achieved.

Zillow, one of the biggest real estate platforms, has leaned heavily into AI for their property valuation. Through the Zestimate tool, the company employs machine learning algorithms utilizing data from different sources, including public records, past sale prices, and current market conditions. The result? A property estimate with a median error rate of merely 1.9%. Importantly, this level of accuracy was achieved after numerous iterations and refinements, highlighting that AI, indeed, learns and improves with time.

6.2. AI-driven Property Searches

AI has started to redefine how property searches are conducted. AI-powered real estate platforms like REX leverage deep learning techniques to provide personalized property recommendations. It provides potential home buyers with tailored suggestions based on their unique preferences and behaviors, streamlining the property search process and offering an unprecedented level of personalization.

In the commercial real estate sector, companies like Cherre employ AI to aggregate and analyze extensive volumes of data, providing realtors, investors, and other stakeholders with actionable insights. Using AI, market trends, property values, and competition levels can be rapidly assessed, providing critical market intelligence that previously would have taken weeks to compile and analyze.

6.3. AI in Real Estate Investment

Investing in real estate has always been a calculated risk. However, firms like Skyline AI are using AI to minimize uncertainties and optimize returns. By employing machine learning, they are able to analyze datasets from various sources, evaluate market trends and forecast property value changes over time. This robust risk analysis often results in safer investments with potentially higher returns.

6.4. Virtual Property Viewing with AI

In the age of social distancing, AI has facilitated a breakthrough in property viewing with the advent of virtual tours. Tech start-up, Matterport, has launched an AI-driven platform that provides 3D walkthroughs of properties, allowing prospective buyers or renters to explore properties from afar. This technology creates a new paradigm where geography is no longer a limitation in real estate.

By leveraging machine learning, the platform can also identify and label the property's features, enriching the viewing experience. It can record and analyze user behavior during the virtual tour, delivering insights to the property owner about what features are particularly liked or disliked by viewers.

6.5. AI in Real Estate: Success Stories

Now let's round off with a focus on two companies that have utilized AI to revolutionize their business model: COMPASS and Opendoor.

COMPASS, a real estate platform, unleashed the potential of AI through a predictive analytics tool named 'Compass Markets'. With this tool, COMPASS tracks market trends, price fluctuations, inventory changes and more, all in real time. One of the key benefits has been an improvement in buyer-seller matchmaking, resulting in accelerated transactions and happy customers.

On the other end of the spectrum are companies like Opendoor, who have harnessed the power of AI to facilitate quicker home selling processes. They employ AI to evaluate home value based on data available from various sources, make an offer within 24 hours, and close a deal in minimal time. This dramatically reduces the time homes spend on the market.

In conclusion, AI's impacts on real estate have been profound and expansive. These triumphs are not just transforming how the real estate industry operates, but also redefining the concept of property ownership and investment. As we continue to unravel the capabilities of AI, the future looks bright, albeit less predictable, and puts one thing beyond doubt - in real estate, AI has just begun marking its territory.

Chapter 7. Challenges and Limitations of AI in Real Estate

As we uncover the potential opportunities and impacts of artificial intelligence (AI) on the real estate industry, it's equally essential to consider the headwinds and limitations that block the full adoption and implementation of AI. While the future prospects are exciting, there remain several challenges and limitations to be mindful of.

7.1. The Complexity of Real Estate

Real estate is a complex world with immense diversity in property types, geographic variations, and market dynamics. Using AI to understand and predict these factors is not straightforward. Each property is unique, and current AI models may not fully account for such individuality. Certain elements, such as the architectural style, neighborhood sentiment, or location-specific factors, such as proximity to key amenities or public transportation, are incredibly nuanced and still difficult for AI systems to completely comprehend.

Quantifying elements like the condition of the property, the aesthetics, and the emotional value potential buyers may associate with it are factors that reside outside the scope of current AI capabilities. Even though technical advancements will continue driving AI's learning and interpreting abilities forward, understanding the subtleties of real estate complexity will remain challenging.

7.2. Data Confidentiality and Security

AI is wholly dependent on data, which brings two significant challenges: confidentiality and security. Real estate deals with highly personal and sensitive information. Protecting this data is paramount, and any breach can lead to severe legal and reputational consequences. Establishing robust data protection measures and ensuring AI systems are shielded against potential cybersecurity threats is a journey, not a destination.

Moreover, consumers and regulators continue to push for stringent data confidentiality and privacy rights. Navigating this landscape while maintaining the efficiency and innovation AI brings calls for deliberate strategizing. AI systems must be designed and trained to comply with data protection laws and treat privacy as a topmost priority.

7.3. The Bias Challenge

The algorithmic models that AI uses can become skewed if the data fed to them is biased, and this is particularly problematic in real estate. Discrimination, whether unintentional or otherwise, can become embedded in AI systems, leading to unfair housing practices. These biases might derive from historical patterns of racial or socio-economic inequalities that are reflected in the data AI systems are trained on.

Ensuring fair, impartial, and ethical use of AI in real estate is a critical challenge. This requires rigorous testing and refinement of AI models, remaining aware of potential biases and ensuring that all algorithmic predictions are equitable and just.

7.4. Technological Infrastructure

While AI promises greater efficiencies in processing and analyzing real estate data, its full implementation requires a strong technological infrastructure. This includes advanced computing power, robust IT support, and complex software, all of which entail significant upfront costs and ongoing maintenance.

Adapting existing systems to integrate AI technology can be a daunting task, requiring significant resources and expertise, and might lead to temporary disruptions in business operations. For smaller organizations in particular, this could be a significant hurdle to overcome.

7.5. Human-AI Interaction

The real estate industry is deeply relationship-driven. Clients value personal interactions and trust developed through human rapport. It's a sector that thrives on negotiation, understanding client aspirations, and guiding them through an emotional journey. While AI can optimize efficiency and provide more informed and accurate predictions, it lacks the human touch.

Striking a balance between technological innovation and maintaining the personal element inherent to real estate transactions is a challenge. Although we can expect AI to take over more functions as it evolves, the importance of human intuition and experience in the real estate industry should not be underestimated.

7.6. Regulatory Concerns

AI's introduction into the real estate sector also brings with it a fresh set of regulatory considerations. Governments worldwide are grappling with how to regulate AI applications while still encouraging innovation. Legislation around issues such as data privacy, housing discrimination, and accountability for AI decisions is still emerging and is often unable to keep pace with the rapid advancements in technology.

This calls for savvy navigation of the regulatory landscape. Organizations adopting AI must not only stay abreast of current laws and regulations but also anticipate potential regulatory shifts.

7.7. The Skill Gap

The integration of AI into the real estate sector necessitates new skill sets that are currently scarce. Understanding AI requires technical knowledge that many real estate professionals do not possess. Hence, there could be a significant learning curve for existing industry professionals, and recruiting new talent may be challenging given the demand for these skills across various sectors.

Training programs to upskill existing employees, and comprehensive strategies to attract and retain AI-versed professionals, are vital for organizations planning to leverage AI in their operations.

Despite the tantalizing promise of AI, it is essential to consider these challenges and limitations during strategic decision-making. AI may not be a silver bullet to all real estate issues, but with careful navigation of these potential roadblocks, its adoption can facilitate a powerful transformation in the industry.

Chapter 8. Exploring the Ethics of AI in Property Management

Artificial Intelligence holds the promise of fundamentally redefining and enhancing the fields of property management and real estate. However, as we increase our application of advanced algorithmic systems and data-driven methodologies, we simultaneously encounter complex ethical challenges that deserve our close attention. So let's delve deep into understanding the ethical elements of AI in property management.

8.1. Transparency and Trustworthiness

When it comes to property management, trust is a crucial component. Tenants, property owners, and regulatory bodies must trust the methods and systems in place to facilitate all property-related activities. As AI becomes increasingly woven into these processes, the need for transparency and openness in these systems increases.

Often, AI's decision-making capabilities are labelled as 'black-box' operations that inhibit understanding and foster suspicion. The opacity of AI algorithms can lead to biased or discriminatory practices. Property management professionals should commit themselves to prioritise transparency. They should make efforts to explain to people involved - tenants, property owners, and local administrative bodies - how AI is being used, how it makes certain decisions, and how their data is being handled.

8.2. Fairness and Bias

AI is only as fair as the data it's trained on. Unfortunately, historical and societal biases have a tendency to be embedded in datasets. Thus, unless explicitly designed to counter these biases, AI can inadvertently perpetuate and amplify discrimination. This could occur in property management when AI is used for activities like tenant screening or property valuation.

For example, an AI system trained on rental history data from a region where racial minorities were historically declined rentals could perpetuate the same bias. Similarly, AI used for property valuations might undervalue homes in lower-income neighborhoods based on historical data.

Fairness needs to be explicitly programmed into AI systems, including by addressing these implicit biases in underlying data. The AI models used should regularly undergo fairness audits and bias checks using statistical methods to ensure compliance with fair housing norms and regulations.

8.3. Privacy and Data Security

AI thrives on data - the more it has, the better it performs. But in the realm of property management, this voracious data appetite could lead to serious privacy and data security concerns.

Is it justified for a property management system to know everything about each tenant's income, lifestyle, habits, or social relationships? Who should have access to this information and for how long? How should it be stored safely? These are questions property managers need to address when embedding AI in their operations.

AI in property management must abide by privacy laws and norms. More importantly, the application of AI should not compromise the basic dignity and privacy rights of individuals involved. Consent and control mechanisms to safeguard data should be built into AI systems. Property managers must ensure that AI providers have robust data security measures to prevent breaches.

8.4. Accountability

In a world where AI systems increasingly drive decisions, who is held accountable when things go wrong? In property management, the consequences could be as dire as unlawful eviction or mistaken property valuation.

In these scenarios, accountability can be hard to define. Is it the property management company, the AI developer, or the data provider who pieced together the training data for the AI model responsible? While the legal domain is yet to catch up with this complex scenario, property managers need to think about designs and contracts that enforce clear responsibility.

Careful planning is required to ensure a clear understanding of who is responsible for what, how remediation will be carried out in case of failures, and the delineations of responsibility between AI provider, property management company and stakeholders.

8.5. Open Societal Debate

Deploying AI in property management also requires an open societal debate. Everyone involved - from tenants and property owners to AI developers and governance bodies - should be active and engaged.

After all, the AI-driven future we are creating will not just impact professionals in real estate or tech, but nearly everyone. Fair housing, sustainable communities, and economic equality are society-wide concerns, not just for a niche industry.

A collective societal discussion is crucial to establish what the most ethical use cases for AI in property management are, how it should be governed, and how to mitigate potential risks.

8.6. Conclusion

Exploring the ethics of AI in property management is no small task; it requires difficult questions and constant re-evaluations. However, as we move forward in this AI-driven world, this is not just necessary but an absolute imperative. Implementing AI with ethical considerations at its core will ensure a future where technology doesn't just make our lives easier, but also fairer and more just.

Chapter 9. The Future of Real Estate: A Forecast with AI

Few technological advancements have infiltrated industry and lifestyle fabrics quite like Artificial Intelligence (AI). From predictive algorithms shaping the ad-targeting on our social media feeds to voice-controlled assistants like Amazon's Alexa or Apple's Siri, AI has become a central and consequential part of our lived experiences. Nowhere is this amalgamation of tradition and modernity more evident than in the realm of real estate. Over the last few years, AI has descended upon real estate practices with a transformative gust, promising efficiencies, accuracies, and vast improvements in decision-making.

9.1. Machine Learning and Predictive Analytics

In the world of real estate, evaluations, and transactions revolve around timely and accurate data. One of the significant AI breakthroughs lies in machine learning leading to highly powerful predictive analytics that can assess performance-related data and glean actionable insights.

AI's iterative capability allows the system to learn from each data interaction, thus improving execution with every experience. Algorithms predict various outcomes based on different variables, such as home price indices, neighborhood demographics, economic indicators, and historical market trends. These predictions provide real estate professionals with valuable insights into market fluctuations and real estate valuations - leading to more tactical decision-making and effective risk management.

However, the application of machine learning and predictive

analytics is not just limited to predicting market trends and property values. They also allow real estate firms to tailor client experiences. For instance, based on a prospective buyer's preferences and behaviors, a predictive algorithm can generate targeted property listing recommendations, reducing search times and increasing client engagement.

9.2. The Rise of PropTech

This digital inundation of real estate is commonly referred to as PropTech (Property Technology), and AI stands as a significant pillar of this revolution. PropTech companies leverage cutting-edge technologies, like big data, AI, and machine learning tools to streamline and innovate traditional real estate practices. As an example, Zillow's "Zestimate," a home-valuation algorithm, reflects the use of AI to provide instant property appraisals.

Other PropTech platforms, like Redfin and Realtor, are continuously improving their recommendation algorithms to offer personalized property matches based on preferences specified by users. This not only simplifies the search process but also increases the probability of closing a sale.

9.3. AI in Investment Strategies

With AI and big data, investors now have a prediction-based model that encompasses a larger spectrum of factors and potential scenarios. This effective tool creates a more accurate forecasting model, creating a clearer path for investors.

AI-driven tools generate in-depth market analysis reports, comparing scores of properties across several parameters and predicting future trends. Investors can use these reports to shape their buying, selling, and holding strategies, leading to improved returns and reduced investment risks.

Another intriguing way AI impacts investment strategies is through robo-advisors. These AI-powered platforms provide users with automated, algorithm-driven financial planning services with minimal human intervention. In the real estate sector, robo-advisors can guide an investor in making informed decisions.

9.4. Automation in Real Estate Transactions

AI has also induced automation in real estate transactions. Several PropTech companies have shifted towards automatic property management systems. These systems, often powered by AI, have changed the way property managers operate. AI can automate various repetitive tasks such as rent collection, maintenance requests handling, and even lease contract management.

Chatbots and AI-enabled virtual assistants are being used in an escalating number to field queries, provide support, and interact with potential buyers or tenants, offering immediate and 24/7 availability. This not only improves customer relations but also allows professionals to focus on high-level tasks that require human oversight.

9.5. The Potential of AI in Real Estate

There's no denying the potential of AI in transforming real estate operations. From enhancing customer experience to enabling better investment decisions, AI is shaping the future of real estate.

However, like any technological voyage, the course isn't without obstacles. As businesses increasingly rely on AI, they must also address concerns related to data privacy and the ethical application of such tools. Despite these challenges, the constant evolution of AI technology is an exciting prospect. The synergy of AI and real estate is the seed to a more efficient, more accessible, and more lucrative property market.

Undoubtedly, the role of AI in real estate is both substantial and impactful. As we navigate the cusp of this new era, we find ourselves standing at a juncture where an established industry meets spectral promises of future technology. This, indeed, is the transformative evolution of property investment. No longer mere conjecture, this reality is here - blending the line between tomorrow's anticipation and today's experiences. Innovation is at the heart of this transformation, and embracing it may well be the key to unlocking a new world of real estate potential.

Chapter 10. Bonus: Expert Views on AI-driven Real Estate

Any industry's future, including real estate, is shaped by the visionaries at its helm. These are the experts, individuals who live and breathe their subject area, who are not just in tune with the future but are often the ones guiding us there. In our bonus chapter, they weigh in on AI in Real Estate.

10.1. The Pioneers of AI in Real Estate

As pioneers in leveraging AI, these individuals have been leading the charge in integrating the technology into the real estate arena. Here, they lend us some insight into how AI could revolutionize property investment.

George Russell, CEO of Russell Properties, underlines AI's capacity to turn significant volumes of structured and unstructured data into sensible, effective decision-making materials.

"Applying AI in redefining our business model has resulted in effective predictions about trends," Russell declares. "By analyzing data from periods with similar economic indicators, AI helps anticipate market behavior with impressive accuracy."

However, it's not enough to have the technologies available. Russell emphasizes a combination approach - leveraging AI, but also nurturing an internal culture that is accepting of these changes. "It's equally necessary to have a team that is excited about AI, as they are the ones who will be using the products daily."

10.2. AI's Impact on Property Valuation

In the realm of property valuation, AI has the potential to redefine approaches and methodologies. Property valuation, traditionally an area fraught with human error and bias, can significantly benefit from AI's precision, objectivity, and continuity. This notion is personified in the vision of Patricia James, Chief Data Scientist at PropVal Analytics.

"We've developed an AI solution that's redefining the property valuation process," James shares. "By training our algorithms on extensive sets of property data, we've reduced the scope for human bias and error. AI engines can consider factors that a human assessor might miss, lending an air of objectivity and precision to property valuations."

10.3. Bringing Transparency to Real Estate

AI's ability to bring transparency in property transactions is another area that Marcus Bowers, a prominent proptech entrepreneur and founder of OpenHouse.AI, strongly advocates.

"Traditionally, many aspects of property transactions have been 'grey areas,' causing mistrust between stakeholders," Bowers says. "AI-powered technologies like blockchain and smart contracts are ensuring visibility into every stage of a transaction, fostering trust in the system."

10.4. AI's Role in Sustainable Real Estate

Eco-conscious investors and property owners take note: AI can also play a pivotal role in sustainable property management. Elizabeth Norman of Green Buildings, Inc. emphasizes this point, sharing, "AI can optimize energy utilization, reducing carbon footprints significantly on a large scale."

Norman explains that AI can analyze patterns and predict energy consumption, allowing for more efficient management of resources. "Not just a game changer for the environment, AI in green real estate could make 'climate risk' a thing of the past for anxious investors," she adds.

10.5. The Future of AI in Real Estate

The future potential of AI in real estate is immeasurable. As Dave Lewis of AI Estate puts it, "The methods and means of real estate are changing, and AI is at the heart of this evolution."

"We're just scratching the surface," he says. "Big Data, Machine Learning, IoT – these are set to propel real estate into the 21st century."

AI, the herald of the 4th industrial revolution, in real estate can promote operational efficiency, improve customer experiences, and enhance decision making. At its core, AI offers a reminder: Transforming the way we buy, sell, and think about property isn't simply a matter of turning towards the future. It's about the benefits that future can bring – for investors, for homeowners, for anyone with a stake in the real estate game.

In the end, these experts elucidate one crucial point - AI isn't just about the technology; it's about the people and the missions they bring to life. It's about real estate professionals becoming more effective, clients having better experiences, and our buildings becoming smarter, more sustainable places to live and work. It's about howAI can make the world a bit better.

Chapter 11. Conclusion: Stealth Revolution - Adapting to AI in Real Estate

The destiny of real estate has intertwined itself irreversibly with the rapidly evolving technology of Artificial Intelligence. As our journey across this vast intersection of technology and tradition winds down, it's worthwhile to pan back, study the transformed landscape and prepare for the future that's already knocking on our doors.

11.1. Evaluating the Impact

The influence of AI on real estate can hardly be overstated. It's propelled upheaval, redesign, and innovation at a pace scarcely imagined a decade ago. From refactoring the subtlest nuances of property valuation with predictive analytics to fomenting entirely new AI-driven investment strategies, AI's imprint is indisputable. AI's continued evolution has recalibrated our understanding of what's possible in real estate, transforming it from a traditional, human-driven business into a space brimming with potential for further change and technological advancement.

Amidst the whirlwind of AI-driven transformation, stakeholders who once held unchallenged mastery in navigating the murky waters of property investments are now compelled to unlearn and relearn the rules of the game. As the integration of AI in real estate accelerates, adaptability is no longer optional—it is an imperative for survival.

11.2. Embracing the Transitions: Learning to Thrive

This new reality necessitates a change in perspective and an acceptance of the shifting landscape. To thrive in this AI-integrated world, there are several areas of adaptability and development both individuals and companies in real estate must focus on.

First, it is paramount to develop a solid understanding of AI and related technologies. While everyone need not be an expert, having a grasp of the basic principles, methodologies, and potential applications of AI can empower decision-making. Knowledge of AI provides an expanded toolkit for real estate professionals, enabling them to analyze markets, estimate property prices and negotiate deals with an enhanced level of insight and precision.

Second, there's a need to nurture an innovation centric culture. AI provides an unveiling array of tools and techniques that need to be studied, understood, and applied strategically. Having an innovation-driven mindset is instrumental in implementing these new features effectively and for seeking out ways AI can augment or enhance existing strategies.

11.3. AI for Problem-solving and Efficiency

A pivotal shift that AI integration brings to the real estate sector is its capabilities to seek out, pinpoint, and neutralize inefficiencies outside the purview of traditional methodologies. From automating time-consuming tasks to providing custom-tailored recommendations to clients based on their unique preferences, AI acts as a catalyst for efficiency and streamlined work processes.

AI, with its intelligent automation and advanced analytical

capabilities, can significantly cut down on the time and resources spent on tasks such as tenant screening, property management, and in-depth market analysis. Embracing these transitions not only enhances operational efficiencies but also facilitates a high-return, high-impact investment environment.

11.4. Ethical Considerations

As AI revolutionizes real estate, it's important to deliberate on the ethical implications that arise. The onus of responsible adoption of AI lays heavily on businesses. Ensuring transparency, fairness and unbiased decision making is fundamental to embracing AI ethically in real estate. Companies should create an ethical governance framework for AI implementation and make a concerted effort to address the risks and societal implications of AI-led decision-making.

11.5. Final Thoughts

We sit at the crest of an era of unprecedented change, where AI is initiating a stealth revolution in real estate. The sector's adaptation to this surge of technology isn't a choice or a trend that can be ignored. It is a wave that will either push the industry toward new heights or engulf those who choose to stand still.

The oft-quoted saying by Louis Pasteur— "Chance favors the prepared mind"—rings true in this context. Early adoption and adaptation to AI in real estate is a testament to both foresight and wisdom. The murmurings of this stealth revolution have transcended to a clear clarion call. It's time to plug in, learn, adapt, and ride the wave of transformation.